Molly's Hard Bargain

story by Janet Craig

illustrations by Barbara Hranilovich

HARCOURT BRACE & COMPANY

Orlando   Atlanta   Austin   Boston   San Francisco   Chicago   Dallas   New York
Toronto   London

Brian loved to make bargains with his little sister Molly.

On Monday it was Brian's turn to walk the dog. "Molly," he said, "let's make a deal. Heads, you win the dime. Tails, you walk the dog."

Brian tossed the dime, and Molly had to walk the dog.

On Tuesday, Mom asked Brian, "Please take out the trash." Brian thought fast.

"Let's play checkers. The loser takes out the trash."

"Okay," said Molly.

Guess who took out
the trash.

It was the same on Wednesday. Brian made a bargain, and Molly had to take her brother's backpack to school.

On Thursday Molly lost a race and had to clean Brian's room.

On Friday, Brian could not find his baseball mitt. "Molly, did you see my baseball mitt?"

"Let's make a deal," she said. "Sign this paper, and I'll help you find your mitt."

Brian read the paper
and signed it.

For the next week, Brian walked the dog, took out the trash, carried Molly's backpack, and did the dishes. He even cleaned his own room.

And he didn't even mind.